WARRIORS

MORITURI TE SALUTAMUS

We, who are about to die, salute you

KINGFISHER

WELCOME TO VS, WHERE THE STAGE IS SET FOR
AN EXTRAVAGANZA OF THE FIERCEST, BLOODIEST,
MOST INCREDIBLE CONTESTS OF ALL TIME.

TEN WARRIORS FROM CENTURIES
PAST CLASH AS NEVER BEFORE,

4 THE WARRIORS

VIKING
AZTEC

VS

ARENA 1

12 VIKING

AZTEC 14

SAMURAI
GLADIATOR

VS

ARENA 2

22 SAMURAI

GLADIATOR 24

KNIGHT
ZULU

VS

ARENA 3

32 KNIGHT

ZULU 34

THE ARENAS

NINJA
GLADIATRIX

VS

ARENA 4

SPARTAN
MONGOL

VS

ARENA 5

When all five battles are over, one victor will be crowned with the greatest honour – history's ultimate warrior!

LET'S MEET THE TEN WARRIORS ▶

SPARTAN 480BCE

From the 8th to the 4th century BCE, the ancient Greek city-state of Sparta was a military superpower. All of its citizens were soldiers – hoplites – whose lives were dedicated to the art of war.

GLADIATRIX 100CE

The female gladiators of ancient Rome, like their male counterparts, were athletes rather than soldiers, fighting in one-to-one contests in the 1st and 2nd century CE for public entertainment.

GLADIATOR 50BCE

In ancient Rome and its empire, contests involving gladiators – well-trained, well-armed athletes who fought in single combat – were hugely popular from the 4th century BCE to the 3rd century CE.

VIKING 840CE

From the late 8th to the 11th century, the Vikings, from Scandinavia, ransacked and conquered much of Europe. Skilful, fierce and determined, Viking warriors were among the most feared fighters of their age.

LOCATION

WARRIOR WORLD

HERE IS THE BATTLE-READY LINE-UP: THE TEN FIGHTERS WHO WILL COMPETE TO BE HISTORY'S ULTIMATE WARRIOR. THEY COME FROM CENTURIES PAST AND FROM AROUND THE GLOBE. MOVE THROUGH THE BOOK AND INTO THE ARENAS, AND PREPARE TO BE AMAZED BY DRAMATIC SCENES OF COMBAT. ALONG THE WAY, CONSULT EACH WARRIOR'S DATA PAGE FOR FACTS ABOUT THE SKILLS AND WEAPONS ON DISPLAY, AND DISCOVER THE HISTORY AND CULTURE THAT SHAPED EACH COMBATANT.

5

MONGOL 1250ce

In the 12th and 13th century, this warlike nomadic people from central Asia amassed the largest empire in history. Mongol warriors were deadly archers – fast, ruthless and cruel.

7

AZTEC 1500ce

The Aztec empire in Mexico thrived from the 12th century until its fall in 1521. Aztec society was centred around warfare and the sacrifice of captured prisoners. All its men were warriors.

8

NINJA 1550ce

From the mid-15th to the 19th century, the ninja were Japan's secret warriors. These martial arts experts were feared and despised by other warriors, but their skills as assassins were indispensable.

6

KNIGHT 1450ce

European knights fought in hundreds of bloody wars from the 9th to the 16th century. These noblemen soldiers had hi-tech weapons and armour, and spent their lives training for battle or waging war.

9

SAMURAI 1580ce

From the 8th to the 19th century, Japan was dominated by the samurai. These noble warrior knights had a strict code of honour and superb fighting methods. Rivalry between samurai clans was fierce.

10

ZULU 1820ce

In the 19th century, the Zulu nation came to prominence in southern Africa. Zulu warriors had basic but deadly weapons, and were aggressive and disciplined fighters, formidable in single combat.

JAGUAR

1. MACUAHUITL (SAW-SWORD)

2. JAGUAR-HEAD HELMET

3. CHIMALLI (SHIELD)

4. TLAHUIZTLI (SUIT OF HONOUR) – FEATHER-COVERED BODYSUIT

5. ICHCAHUIPILLI (QUILTED COTTON ARMOUR, WORN UNDERNEATH THE TLAHUIZTLI)

1550 CE

DATA FILE

AZTEC WARRIORS TOOK THOUSANDS OF CAPTIVES AS THEY ADVANCED THROUGH MEXICO IN THE 15TH CENTURY. IN BATTLE A WARRIOR'S GOAL WAS TO MAIM AND CAPTURE HIS FOE. EACH CAPTURE BROUGHT HIM HONOUR AND STATUS. THE JAGUARS WERE ONE OF SEVERAL ELITE WARRIOR SOCIETIES.

PICK A WEAPON

AXE
This weapon is heavy (over 4kg). It may be basic, but it can still do real damage when swung at an enemy's head.

ATLATL
Use this throwing stick along with a dart or spear. It takes a lot of skill, but will kill at a distance.

MACUAHUITL
This precision instrument is a 1m-long wooden sword inlaid with razor-sharp pieces of obsidian (natural glass). Use it to slice and slash – to maim, dismember or even decapitate.

ADD STAMINA

FOOD
Keep fighting fit with the protein-rich Aztec staple diet of maize, beans and squash – and an invigorating chilli chocolate drink.

FIRST AID
Treat wounds with poultices, salves and disinfectants, made from aloes, cactus juice and urine, and prepared by healers.

ADVICE
Take heart from knowing that, at home, your father is making daily offerings to the god of your birthday to ensure your safety in combat.

MAKE YOUR MOVE

CHARGE!
Run at your enemy at full speed to stun him by body impact.

ATTACK
Wave your macuahuitl fiercely, swinging as fast and furiously as you can.

PARRY
Defend with the shield while slashing at the enemy's arms and legs.

AZTEC

VIKING

DATA FILE

FROM THE LATE 8TH TO THE 11TH CENTURY, THE VIKINGS WENT FORTH FROM THEIR LANDS IN SCANDINAVIA TO CONQUER MUCH OF EUROPE. LITHSMEN WERE FREE WARRIORS, SWORN TO SERVE THEIR LEADERS UNTO DEATH IN RETURN FOR FOOD, GOLD AND LAND.

VS

LITHSMAN

1. LONGSWORD
2. 'SPECTACLE' HELMET
3. WOOLLEN TUNIC
4. SCABBARD
5. ROUND WOODEN SHIELD WITH IRON BOSS IN THE CENTRE

840CE

PICK A WEAPON

SHIELD
This warshield, with its heavy iron boss, can be smashed into an opponent's head. Many lined up together make a solid advancing wall.

AXE
This broad-bladed axe is wielded with one or both hands, and is a powerful weapon to choose for a duel. It can deliver a skull-shattering blow to the enemy.

LONGSWORD
This 1m-long, double-edged steel sword is the Viking warrior's most prized possession. Longswords are passed down from father to son.

MAKE YOUR MOVE

DOUBLE STRIKE
Close in with the shield to prevent being hit, and strike hard with the axe.

SHIELD STRIKE
Smash the shield into the head, chest or weapon arm before slashing.

HIGH STRIKE
Whirl the axe around to confuse, then bring it down with great force.

FOOD
Look forward to a victory meal of roast meat with a celebratory drink of beer or mead – better than your daily fare of porridge and cheese.

FIRST AID
When wounded, eat an onion-and-herb porridge. If the wound starts to smell of onion, then – WARNING! – you may well die.

ADVICE
Take pride in your battle-dress to intimidate the enemy. Keep hair and beard groomed, clean out ear wax and wear fine clothes and jewellery.

ADD STAMINA

VIKING

THE JAGUAR WARRIOR LIES VANQUISHED

THE VIKING WINS

THE VIKING WINS, WITH A BLOW OF HIS HEAVY BATTLEAXE. HE IS WELL TRAINED IN INDIVIDUAL COMBAT, HAS LONG EXPERIENCE OF THIS KIND OF FIGHTING AND IS KNOWN FOR HIS FEROCITY AND SKILL IN A DUEL. HE IS BIGGER AND STRONGER THAN THE AZTEC, AND WILL WIN HONOUR FROM SLAYING THE ENEMY. THE AZTEC FIGHTS IN A VERY DIFFERENT WAY. HE HAS BEEN TRAINED TO CAPTURE PRISONERS FOR SACRIFICE, RATHER THAN TO KILL THEM. HE SLASHES HAPHAZARDLY WITH HIS MACUAHUITL, BUT IS NO MATCH FOR THE VIKING.

VIKING

BATTLEAXE AND A NOBLE WARRIOR'S LONGSWORD

KNOWN AS NORTHMEN OR SEA WOLVES, THE VIKINGS SET SAIL FROM SCANDINAVIA FROM ABOUT 1,200 YEARS AGO. FEARED WARRIORS, THEY STORMED ALONG THE COASTS AND RIVERS OF EUROPE, IN SEARCH OF LAND AND PLUNDER.

LONGSHIP RAIDERS

The sight of a Viking sail on the horizon struck terror into many hearts. Each longship was fast and sleek, yet shallow enough to sail down a river or be dragged up a beach. Its prow was carved like a snarling dragon's head. Each longship carried 30 or more battle-scarred warriors, heavily armed and ready to fight. They burned down monasteries, churches and towns, seizing gold, jewellery, cattle or slaves.

SILVER ARM-RING

BERSERKER!

This chess piece shows a Viking biting his shield in fury. He is a berserker. Berserkers were warriors from a particular cult, who worked themselves into a frenzied rage before a battle. They wore bearskin shirts, fought without armour and were said not to feel pain. Today we still talk about people 'going berserk', or crazy.

A BLAZE OF GLORY

A Viking longship is set on fire at a festival in Shetland, UK. Vikings fought in Ireland, the British Isles, France and southern Europe. They served as bodyguards in Byzantium (now Istanbul) and traded in Russia and the Middle East. They settled in Iceland and Greenland, and even reached North America.

HEROES IN VALHALLA

INTO BATTLE

Vikings mostly fought in small bands, but sometimes joined forces as an army. They were not highly organized, but were strong, bloodthirsty and well armed, with lethal swords and battleaxes, bows and spears. They carried shields made of wood and iron. Most wore simple tunics and cloaks, and helmets of metal or leather, but a jarl (rich chieftain) or hersir (noble warrior) might wear a fine shirt of mail, and a metal helmet to protect the face.

WARLIKE GODS

The first Vikings worshipped gods who were believed to be just as violent as they were. Warriors who died bravely in battle were thought to go to Valhalla, the great hall of the gods. Odin, father of the gods, rode through the sky on an eight-legged horse. He had two ravens that could fly around the world. Odin's raven emblem was a sight to bring fear to the Vikings' enemies. Although they were strong in battle, the Vikings usually overcame their enemies in fierce surprise attacks and secret raids.

ACTORS RECREATE A VIKING ATTACK ON LINDISFARNE, UK, THAT TOOK PLACE IN 793CE.

ATTACK FORCE

13

FOUR CAPTURES. THE CENTRE WARRIOR, WITH AN EAGLE MOTIF ON HIS SHIELD, HAS MADE FIVE. ON THE RIGHT IS A JAGUAR WARRIOR.

HONOUR THROUGH CAPTURE

A WARRIOR GAINED PROMOTION WHEN HE CAPTURED AN ENEMY SINGLE-HANDED AND BROUGHT THE PRISONER HOME FOR SACRIFICE. HE WAS GIVEN A SPECIAL FORM OF BATTLE-DRESS TO MARK THIS ACHIEVEMENT. AFTER MAKING FIVE CAPTURES, A WARRIOR MIGHT JOIN ONE OF THE ELITE FIGHTING UNITS.

STRANGE INVADERS

The Aztecs were the most powerful people in 15th-century Mexico. They defeated many enemies, but in 1519 the Spanish invaded. The pale-skinned strangers had horses, ships, guns and swords. They did not fight by any of the Aztec rules of war. In 1521 the Aztec capital, Tenochtitlán, was besieged, and over 240,000 warriors died in three months of bitter fighting. The Aztec empire was crushed.

AZTEC

AZTEC WARRIOR WITH HEADDRESS

WHEN AN AZTEC BOY WAS BORN, HIS FIRST PRESENT WAS A BOW AND ARROW. HE WAS DESTINED FROM BIRTH TO BE A WARRIOR. A GRUESOME FATE AWAITED THOSE WHOM HE DEFEATED IN BATTLE...

TRAINING FOR WAR

HOW TO BECOME A WARRIOR

In the Aztec empire in the 15th century, all Aztec boys, whether nobles or commoners, started their warrior training at school. They learned how to obey orders, use weapons and fight in battle. Aged 18 they were sent to watch a kind of ritual battle with other tribes, known as a Flower War. When the next Flower War took place they would take part, and risk capture and sacrifice by the enemy. Once they had taken a prisoner themselves, they could become full Aztec warriors, fighting in real battles.

GLADIATOR

MURMILLO

1. GLADIUS (SHORT SWORD)

2. BRONZE HELMET WITH VISOR

3. TALL, RECTANGULAR, CURVED SHIELD

4. GREAVE (METAL LEG PROTECTOR)

5. MANICA (ARM GUARD)

50BCE

DATA FILE

CRIMINALS, SLAVES AND PRISONERS OF WAR ALL LOST THEIR LIVES IN THE BLOODY ARENAS OF ANCIENT ROME FROM 300BCE TO 300CE. THESE WERE THE GLADIATORS. AGED ONLY 18–25, THEY FOUGHT AND EVEN DIED IN ELABORATE SHOWS, STAGED TO ENTERTAIN THE ROMAN CROWDS.

PICK A WEAPON

DAGGER
Although not as powerful a weapon as a sword, a steel dagger is a small, lightweight and useful back-up weapon.

GLADIUS
The gladius, after which the gladiator takes his name, is a short, double-edged sword. Light but deadly, it's perfect for hand-to-hand combat.

TRIDENT
WARNING! Tridents are for retiarii only! These gladiators fight with a net weighted by pieces of lead. They snare their victim under the net, then stab with the three-pronged trident.

ADD STAMINA

FOOD
Eat plenty of boiled beans, dried fruit or barley for strength and to build up fat – it will give you some protection against sword blows.

FIRST AID
You can expect treatment from the best doctors and surgeons available – if you manage to get out of the arena alive!

ADVICE
For some last-minute tips on how to survive the fight, speak to the 'doctor', an ex-gladiator who trains fighters at the gladiator school.

MAKE YOUR MOVE

BLOCK
Thrust the shield forwards to prevent the attacker advancing on you.

ATTACK
Charge, sword raised, but remember to shield your unarmoured body!

DEFEND
Crouch behind the shield to dodge and hide from the enemy's blows.

POWER BAR

THE END OF AN AGE

Weapons like these were used at Aztec royal ceremonies. They included the atlatl, used to hurl pointed darts with great force, and decorative shields of gold and feathers. Aztec warriors fought in battle with bows and arrows, spears, slings, clubs and the macuahuitl. They wore armour of cotton padding. Unlike their enemies the Spanish conquistadores, they had no steel for swords or helmets.

GOLD ATLATL
AND KING
MOTECUHZOMA'S
DECORATED SHIELD

BRINGING HOME THE WAR

The Aztecs believed their gods needed constant offerings, including human lives. Warriors had to prove their worth by presenting prisoners, in their thousands, to be sacrificed to the gods. At the great temple in the centre of Tenochtitlán, Aztec priests cut out prisoners' living hearts with a ceremonial knife. Blood poured down the steps. To the Aztecs, being chosen for sacrifice to the gods was not considered to be cruel or unjust, but a great honour. The scene below shows people acting out a sacrifice as part of a festival.

SAMURAI

THE SAMURAI WINS

THE MURMILLO USUALLY FIGHTS HEAVILY-ARMED GLADIATORS SUCH AS THE THRAEX OR HOPLOMACHUS, SO CAN CHALLENGE THE TAKEDA CLAN WARRIOR. BUT THE SAMURAI'S SUPERIOR BODY ARMOUR ALLOWS HIM TO TAKE MORE RISKS, AND HE MAKES REPEATED CUTS WITH THE FINE BLADE OF HIS SWORD. THE GLADIATOR HAS BEEN TRAINED FOR A CROWD-PLEASING FIGHT AND HIS SHOWY MOVES ARE EASY TO PREDICT. HE IS FORCED ONTO THE DEFENSIVE AND THE SAMURAI SLASHES AT HIS UNARMOURED TORSO AND LEGS. IT IS A CONVINCING SAMURAI VICTORY.

THE GLADIATOR IS DEFEATED

TWO SAMURAI IN PITCHED BATTLE

SAMURAI

IN MEDIEVAL JAPAN, ONLY THE SAMURAI WERE PERMITTED TO CARRY WEAPONS. THEY LIVED BY A WARRIOR'S CODE – THE BUSHIDO – AND SERVED A DAIMYO MASTER IN RETURN FOR PAYMENT AND SHELTER.

RISE OF THE SAMURAI

FROM SERVANTS TO WARRIORS

Between 1603 and 1868, under the rule of the Tokugawa shoguns, all Japanese people belonged to four classes – samurai, farmers, craftspeople and merchants. Within this social structure, the daimyo lords (the top ranks of the samurai class) became very powerful. They had a responsibility to keep the peace, and employed samurai warriors to help them do so. The samurai therefore rose to a high level in society, similar to that of knights in medieval Europe, and are still depicted as heroes in Japanese films and literature today.

POWER BAR

SAMURAI

DATA FILE

FROM THE 8TH TO THE 19TH CENTURY, NOBLE WARRIORS WAGED WAR AMONG THE TRIBAL CLANS OF JAPAN. THEY WERE THE SAMURAI, HIGHLY SKILLED IN HORSE-RIDING, ARCHERY AND DEADLY SWORDPLAY. THEY WERE FIERCE FIGHTERS WHO LIVED BY A WARRIOR CODE, THE BUSHIDO.

TAKEDA CLAN

1. HELMET WITH NECK GUARD
2. KATANA (SWORD)
3. DO (BODY ARMOUR) OF CORDED LEATHER STRIPS
4. SUNEATE (SHIN GUARD)
5. WARAJI (BAMBOO SANDALS) AND PADDED SOCKS

1580CE

PICK A WEAPON

KATANA
The standard fighting sword is the katana. Long and curved, it has one razor-sharp cutting edge and a long handle for two hands to grip.

YARI
The yari (spear), which ranges from 1–6m long, has a sharp steel blade. Samurai carry short, light yari on horseback and use them to stab at their enemy.

TANTO
This small, double-edged dagger, tied to the belt or hidden inside the armour, is used for stabbing or slashing in close combat.

MAKE YOUR MOVE

FURIKABURI
Raise the sword, keeping it horizontal as you do so, and prepare to attack.

NUKIT SUKE
Use the sword to block an attack – the samurai never carry shields.

KIRI OROSHI
Finish an opponent with a fast, powerful downward cut.

ADD STAMINA

FOOD
Before battle, eat dried chestnuts – a sign of victory – with some strength-giving seaweed, shellfish and a drink of sake (rice wine).

FIRST AID
Mash up some daffodil roots into a paste and apply this healing mixture to a sword wound.

ADVICE
Follow the Bushido warrior code that tells you "To die when it is right to die; to strike when it is right to strike."

SAMURAI

Bushido: The Way of the Warrior

"Death shows greater nobility than capture or surrender."

"A samurai warrior must show no interest in material goods and wealth."

CASTLE KEEPS
The powerful Japanese daimyos built large castles. This enabled them to stamp their authority on the surrounding countryside, which they would dominate – and often terrorize – through the activities of their samurai warriors. By demonstrating their military power, and increasing fear across the land, the samurai kept the peace.

RITUAL SUICIDE
Hari-kiri, or stomach-cutting, was a way for Japanese warriors to die voluntarily. Originally, this was only performed by the samurai on themselves, as part of their Bushido heroic code. It allowed them to die with honour rather than fall into the hands of the enemy. It was also used as capital punishment, if a warrior had brought shame upon himself.

THE AGE OF THE WARRING STATES
The Sengoku, or Warring States, period was a time of massive social change, political difficulty and almost constant military conflict in Japan. It lasted from the middle of the 15th century to the beginning of the 17th century. During this period, many samurai lost their lives fighting for their daimyo masters.

CONFLICT

GLADIATOR

HOW COULD THE SCUM OF THE EARTH WIN FAME AND FORTUNE IN ANCIENT ROME? BY PROVING THEIR BRAVERY IN THE ARENA, AS GLADIATORS. THERE WAS JUST ONE PROBLEM – HOW TO SURVIVE...

TRIDENT, USED BY A RETIARIUS

HELMET OF A MURMILLO GLADIATOR

PREPARATION

WHO BECAME A GLADIATOR?

Gladiators were usually the lowest of the low. They might be slaves, criminals or prisoners of war. A few free Romans sometimes chose to fight as gladiators too. Gladiators who managed to stay alive and please the crowd became hugely popular, like sports celebrities today. They could win big prizes and even be presented with their freedom, symbolized by a wooden sword. Once freed, they might become a trainer in a ludus.

LIFE IN THE LUDUS

A gladiator school was called a ludus. It was often next to the amphitheatre where the fights took place. There were barracks where the gladiators slept, rested and ate special meals to build up their strength. In the exercise area, the gladiators would be worked hard under the watchful eye of the owner, or lanista. They were taught how to stab and slash with a short sword, how use the shield and net and spear, how to put on a show, and how to die heroically.

THIS GLADIATOR FROM A FILM OF 2000 IS UNREALISTIC, BUT VERY DRAMATIC!

GLADIATOR TYPES

Several distinct types of gladiator entered the arena. This mosaic shows (from left to right): a retiarius, secutor, thraex, murmillo, hoplomachus and another murmillo. Each had his own type of weapons and armour, and his own way of fighting. The secutor, or 'follower', carried a shield and sword. He would fight against the retiarius, or 'net man', armed with a trident. The murmillo wore an ornate helmet, while the thraex (Thracian) fought with a small, round shield and dagger. The fighters clashed and the crowd bellowed.

DEATH OR GLORY

THE CRUEL ARENA

Amphitheatres were built in hundreds of towns across the Roman empire. On a day when gladiator shows were held, these stadiums would fill with spectators eager to watch the action. Gladiators would fight in pairs. The most spectacular and cruellest gladiator fights were held in the Colosseum in Rome. It could seat 50,000 spectators.

GLADIATOR REBEL

Spartacus (c. 109–71BCE) made his name by leaving the arena for the battlefield. He had been a soldier and a slave before being sold into a ludus. He and his fellow gladiators joined forces and fought their way to freedom. Soon they headed an army of perhaps 140,000 runaway slaves and outlaws. Eventually they were defeated by the Roman army.

1. HELMET WITH HINGED VISOR

2. BEVOR (NECK PROTECTOR)

3. SOLLERET (FOOT PART OF ARMOUR)

4. LONGSWORD

5. SUIT OF ARMOUR, MADE FROM STEEL PLATES JOINED TOGETHER

EARL

1450CE

DATA FILE

THE KNIGHTS OF MEDIEVAL EUROPE WERE A POWERFUL WARRIOR CLASS WHO FOUGHT ON HORSEBACK AND ON FOOT FROM THE 9TH TO THE MID-16TH CENTURY. ENCASED IN ARMOUR AND ARMED WITH MIGHTY SWORDS, THEY DEDICATED THEIR LIVES TO SEEKING VICTORY AND GLORY IN BATTLE.

PICK A WEAPON

POLEAXE
This war-hammer is an essential weapon. Strike with the front or back of the 'hammer' head, or launch a deadly thrust with the spike on top.

LIGHT MACE
This spiked club can be wielded from horseback or in foot-combat, and is designed to smash through armour and cause serious injury.

LONGSWORD
This superb weapon has a double-edged steel blade that is straight and flexible. Use it to slash or stab – it can even pierce metal armour.

ADD STAMINA

FIRST AID
Clean wounds with vinegar. Apply a potion of garlic to reduce the risk of infection, or a balm made from the herb yarrow, to stem bleeding.

ADVICE 1
Take heart from the thought that your stamina is excellent – you've trained to wear your heavy armour for many hours at a time.

ADVICE 2
Always follow the chivalric code of honour. Be fierce, brave and merciless in battle, but courteous and well-mannered to others.

MAKE YOUR MOVE

FRONTAL WARD
This forward position allows you to thrust, cut or deflect from any angle.

HALF-SWORDING
Hold the blade halfway down its length to block or close in, hit and stab.

HIGH WARD
Make devastating blows in any direction, even from beneath your foe.

KNIGHT

ZUL

DATA FILE
ARMED WITH DEADLY WEAPONS AND BOASTING A SOPHISTICATED MILITARY ORGANIZATION, THE ZULU NATION WAS A FORMIDABLE FORCE IN 19TH-CENTURY SOUTHERN AFRICA. AN IQAWE WAS A GREAT WARRIOR AND RENOWNED HERO FROM AMONG THE ZULU FIGHTERS.

PICK A WEAPON

ISIJULA
Use this throwing spear with great accuracy and speed to wound an enemy's torso or pierce a shield from nearly 30m away.

IKLWA
This heavy-bladed war weapon is named after the sucking sound it makes when pulled out of the enemy's flesh. Aim at the stomach.

IWISA
This club is beautifully crafted from a single piece of wood, but its purpose is not pretty – you can use it to beat an enemy's brains out.

VS

IQAWE

1. IKLWA (STABBING SPEAR)
2. ISIJULA (THROWING SPEAR)
3. NECKLACE, WORN AS A PROTECTIVE CHARM
1820CE
4. ISINENE (ANIMAL TAILS)
5. ISIHLANGU (WAR SHIELD, MADE OF COWHIDE)

MAKE YOUR MOVE

DISTRACT
Move the shield and spear back and forth to distract and confuse your enemy.

QUICK THROW
When your enemy is off guard, quickly grab and throw the isijula at him.

THRUST
Deliver a powerful under-arm thrust to the torso with the iklwa.

FOOD

Eat up your beef rations – you'll have more of this nutritious food when serving in the army than at any time in civilian life.

FIRST AID

Bind wounds with grass until you can see the inyanga (healer), who will wash and stitch your wounds and give you powerful medicines.

ADVICE

Ensure the protection of ancestral spirits by taking part in rituals, staged by an inyanga, before battle.

ADD STAMINA

THE KNIGHT WINS

THE ZULU WEARS NEITHER ARMOUR NOR HELMET. HE LACKS A DEVASTATING WEAPON SUCH AS A METAL SWORD OR MACE. A ZULU WARRIOR IS DISCIPLINED AND USES CLEVER TACTICS IN BATTLE, BUT IS LESS SUITED TO A SINGLE-COMBAT CHALLENGE. THE HEAVILY-ARMOURED KNIGHT IS A PROFESSIONAL FIGHTER, WHO HAS PRACTISED SWORDSMANSHIP EVERY DAY FROM A YOUNG AGE. HE HAS BEEN TRAINED TO USE A RANGE OF WEAPONS AND TO MEET A VARIETY OF FIGHTING STYLES IN WHATEVER OPPONENT HE HAS TO FACE.

THE ZULU WARRIOR IS BEATEN

KNIGHT

THE HISTORY OF MEDIEVAL EUROPE WAS MADE BY ARMOURED HORSEMEN, LOYAL TO THEIR LORD AND GREEDY FOR LAND AND POWER. A KNIGHT'S LIFE WAS ONE OF PERMANENT READINESS FOR BATTLE.

WAR CHARGE!

 In the turmoil of battle, a knight and his powerful warhorse would act together. Mounted knights, charging through enemy lines, were vital in battle. From around the 9th to the 16th century CE, European knights fought countless bloody wars, including the Crusades (a series of invasions of lands in the Middle East) and wars between nations, such as France and England's Hundred Years War.

FROM THE CODE OF CHIVALRY:
• FEAR GOD
• SERVE YOUR LORD •
• RESPECT WOMEN
• PROTECT THE WEAK
• HONOUR YOUR FELLOW KNIGHTS
• LIVE BY HONOUR AND FIGHT FOR GLORY

LONGSWORD c. 1300
AND MACE (METAL CLUB)

MEN OF STEEL

These knights wear coats and leggings of mail, made up of interlinking rings of iron. Their helmets or 'great helms' are like buckets, covering the whole head. During the 1300s, knights began to protect some parts of the body with solid metal plates. The emblems on the shield and on the cloth tunic, or surcoat, are called coats-of-arms. These identify each knight in the heat of battle.

MASSIVE WALLS

Kings, lords and knights lived in great castles, with high stone walls. Their aim was to control the surrounding region. Enemies would attack the castle by surrounding it and cutting off supplies – a siege. This castle was built at Conwy, Wales, UK, in the 1280s, after the English king Edward I (reigned 1272–1307), invaded Wales.

THE TOURNAMENT

Tournaments were mock battles, at which knights would practise their fighting skills in combat with one another. They were also festivals of chivalry. The knights showed off to the ladies, and wore fancy armour and plumed helmets. Stories and poems were written about the heroic deeds of knights in battle and at tournaments.

KNIGHTS ON
THE ATTACK,
c. 1250

ARMOUR MADE
FOR A SAXON
(GERMAN)
PRINCE, 1591

HI-TECH ARMOUR

PLATE ARMOUR

By the 1420s, knights wore suits of plate armour, which protected the whole body. The closely fitted sections of steel were joined to each other and the body by leather straps, allowing impressive flexibility of movement despite the heavy weight. Helmets had visors, which could be raised for better vision. The best suits of armour were custom-made for kings and princes, and cost a fortune.

ZULU

DURING THE 1800S, FEW SOUTHERN AFRICAN WARRIORS COULD WITHSTAND THE ONSLAUGHT OF THE ZULU ARMIES. ONCE A PEACEFUL FARMING PEOPLE, THE ZULUS EMERGED AS A POWERFUL FORCE – ORGANIZED AND EXTREMELY AGGRESSIVE.

UTIMUNI, A NEPHEW OF KING SHAKA, IN 1849

NECKLACE OF BONE IN THE SHAPE OF LION CLAWS, WORN BY ROYAL WARRIORS

BATTLE PREPARATION

Zulu armies were trained to march at great speed. Warriors prepared for battle by taking part in a cleansing and strengthening ritual – young warriors would kill a black bull with their bare hands, before roasting and sharing the meat. They were strengthened during battle by snuff (powdered tobacco) containing potent herbs. They slit open the stomachs of their defeated enemies, to allow their spirits to escape. This ritual was called the 'washing of the spears'.

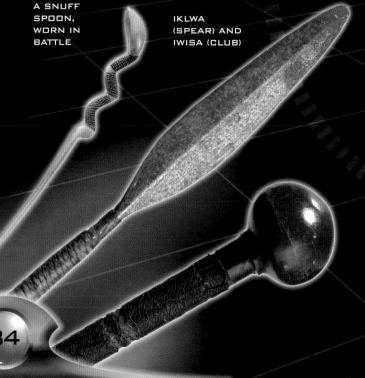

A SNUFF SPOON, WORN IN BATTLE

IKLWA (SPEAR) AND IWISA (CLUB)

KING SHAKA

Shaka (c. 1787–1828) was the most warlike Zulu king. He attacked other tribes and built up a powerful empire. He introduced new weapons, such as the iklwa, a long-headed stabbing spear, and a heavier war shield (isihlangu). He perfected a battle tactic known as the 'horns of the buffalo': his main group of warriors would face the enemy while two flanking groups closed in from the sides and a fourth group waited for the final, fatal onslaught.

TOUGH AND READY

A Zulu fighting group was called an impi. Boys were trained for combat when still young and warriors learned to endure pain by stamping – barefoot – on thorns. From the age of 20, men enlisted in a regiment (iButho) of 1,000 warriors. They were not permanent soldiers but would be called up in the event of war. Shaka could call upon around 20,000 trained fighters.

THE WAR SHIELD WAS ISSUED TO A SOLDIER FIGHTING FOR THE KING.

ZULU WARS

In the 1860s and '70s the Zulus clashed with European invaders, such as Afrikaner settlers and British soldiers, who had modern firearms. In 1879 King Cetshwayo, a nephew of Shaka, went to war. His warriors defeated a British army at Isandlwana. Some Zulus had by then acquired firearms, but their success was due more to surprise, tactics and numbers. The shocked British defeated the Zulus at Ulundi later that year.

" They were giving vent to no loud war-cries, but to a low musical murmuring noise, which gave the impression of a gigantic swarm of bees getting nearer and nearer. "

A Zulu army approaches, from an eye-witness account of the battle of Isandlwana (1879)

HISTORIANS RE-ENACT THE BATTLE OF ISANDLWANA, SOUTH AFRICA.

INVASION

POWER BAR

KUNOICHI

1. COWL (HEAD AND FACE COVERING)

2. KUSARIGAMA

3. SHURIKEN (THROWING STAR)

4. HOKODE (HAND CLAWS)

5. TUNIC AND NARROW TROUSERS MADE FROM VERY DARK BLUE (ALMOST BLACK) CLOTH

1550CE

DATA FILE
LITTLE IS KNOWN FOR SURE ABOUT THE NINJA, SECRET ASSASSINS WHO FOUGHT AND KILLED IN JAPAN FROM AROUND THE MID-15TH TO THE 19TH CENTURY. SKILLED IN MARTIAL ARTS, WITH MANY OF THEIR WEAPONS ADAPTED FROM EVERYDAY FARM AND HOUSEHOLD TOOLS, THEY WERE UNPREDICTABLE ENEMIES.

PICK A WEAPON

SHURIKEN
These throwing stars, hidden in a pocket, are small but deadly. Thrown with spin and speed, they can give your enemy a fatal cut.

KUSARIGAMA
This is made up of a chain, sickle and heavy ball. Entangle your opponent by hurling the ball at her, then strike with the sickle blade.

TESSEN
This feminine-looking object looks like a normal fan, but its concealed iron blades make it a menacing defensive weapon.

ADD STAMINA

FOOD
Carry a 'hunger ball' made from carrots, different kinds of flour, liquorice root and yams preserved in sake (rice wine).

ADVICE 1
Dodge your opponent's sword blows by leaping over the blade and high in the air – so high that she might think you can fly!

ADVICE 2
Seishin teki kyoyo, or spiritual discipline, is the first skill of the ninja. Control yourself and you can control the enemy.

MAKE YOUR MOVE

LEAP
Jump high in the air to give more force as you strike with the sickle.

THROW
Fire the shuriken with precision to cut your opponent down.

CREEP
Move silently with shinso usagi-aruki ('deep grass rabbit walking').

NINJA

GLADIATRIX

GLADIATRIX

DATA FILE

ANCIENT ROMAN SOLDIERS SOMETIMES FACED FEMALE WARRIORS. FROM ABOUT 200BCE TO 200CE, WOMEN INCLUDING CELTS FROM THE NORTH AND NUBIANS FROM AFRICA TOOK TO THE ARENAS IN GLADIATORIAL CONTESTS. WOMEN FIGHTERS BOTH FASCINATED AND APPALLED THE ROMAN PUBLIC.

PICK A WEAPON

PUGIO
This broad-bladed dagger has a sharp point for stabbing with. It is a favourite gladiator weapon, good for close combat.

SICA
This 40cm-long curved dagger, also used by Thracian gladiators, should be aimed at the enemy's unarmoured back.

WOODEN SWORD
Use this wooden version of the gladius in training, to practise your sword skills without getting hurt.

NUBIAN

1. DECORATED METAL BREASTPLATE
2. RECTANGULAR WOODEN SHIELD
100CE
3. PUGIO (DAGGER)
4. ARM PADDING MADE FROM LINEN TIED WITH LEATHER STRIPS
5. BRONZE GREAVES

MAKE YOUR MOVE

DEFEND
Keep the shield in front of you and the dagger raised away from your body.

ATTACK
Move forwards with your right arm raised, ready to stab sharply downwards.

WARM UP
Get psyched up for a fight with a few quick practice moves before you clash.

FOOD
Eat a handful of figs or dates just before you go into the arena – these high-energy foods will give you a much-needed boost.

ADVICE 1
Your daily weapons training should keep you fit and strong, building your stamina for a gruelling fight and sharpening your reflexes.

ADVICE 2
Pray to Anubis, the Egyptian god who leads souls to the afterlife and is also believed to look after fallen gladiators.

ADD STAMINA

POWER BAR

THE GLADIATRIX HAS LOST

THE NINJA WINS

THE GLADIATRIX HAS BEEN TRAINED TO FIGHT IN PUBLIC, AGAINST A FOE OF EQUAL STRENGTH. HER AGILITY AND BATTLE STAMINA ARE GOOD AND HER WEAPONS ARE WELL SUITED TO THE DUEL. THE KUNOICHI USUALLY MURDERS BY STEALTH, IN THE DEAD OF NIGHT, BUT IS AN EXPERT SWORDSWOMAN WHO ADAPTS WELL TO OPEN HAND-TO-HAND FIGHTING. SHE CREATES AN ADVANTAGE BY FORCING THE GLADIATRIX OFF BALANCE BEFORE SHE HAS CHANCE TO FOCUS. THE NINJA JUMPS HIGH IN THE AIR AND STRIKES WITHOUT HESITATION.

NINJA

A SHADOW SLIPS ACROSS A CASTLE WALL. A FIGURE LEAPS FROM A TOWER. BEFORE A JAPANESE WARLORD CAN EVEN REACH THE BATTLEFIELD, HE LIES MURDERED BY MYSTERIOUS ATTACKERS. JUST WHO ARE THESE NINJA?

A SHARP-EDGED THROWING STAR, OR SHURIKEN, WAS ONE OF THE NINJA'S SECRET WEAPONS.

NINJA SWORD (KATANA)

THE SECRET KILLERS

 ### NINJUTSU

A modern re-enactment, staged in Japan, shows how ninja scaled a castle wall, commando-style. Ninjutsu means 'the art of stealth'. Ninja were trained to do the jobs that samurai were not permitted to do because of their code of honour, the Bushido. Male ninjas were trained in assassination, concealment, spying, burglary, diversionary tactics and dirty tricks. Female ninja, or kunoichi, were experts in disguise and poisoning. Ninja were the unseen enemy.

A NINJA COULD PERFORM IMPRESSIVE FEATS OF ACROBATICS.

DANGEROUS LADIES

Often a kunoichi might disguise herself as a noblewoman, a maidservant or a geisha, and use feminine customs as a cover for murder. She might kill with poison in a guest's tea, blades concealed in her fan, or the extra-sharp point of a hairpin. Or she might simply listen and smile as a powerful lord discussed his battle plans, and memorize everything.

THE NINJA CULT

Today many people are fascinated by ninja. Male and female ninja feature in Japanese, Chinese and international popular culture – in films, comic books and computer games. We don't know a great deal about these secretive fighters, so there is a lot of scope for fantasy and invention. These fighters wear bright scarlet and we can see their graceful acrobatics, but ninja probably wore very dark clothes, to help them hide.

WHO WERE THE NINJA?

Much of the history of the ninja has been romanticized. However, ninja warriors, also known as shinobi, and women spies and assassins, really did exist. They were probably active in Japan from the mid-15th century, for about 300 years. The Iga and Koga provinces were the centres of activity. Ninja were widely feared as assassins, but their most useful skills were probably getting into castles during a siege or scouting behind enemy lines.

As well as the standard gladiator shows, Roman arenas staged mock sea battles, the baiting and slaughter of wild animals, and the execution of prisoners. Organizers were always looking for a new act or spectacle to shock and thrill the public. From 63CE onwards, women were sometimes being taken on as gladiators: to fight from chariots or to face each other in single combat, or as venatores (who fought wild animals). Many people thought that female gladiator shows were scandalous. Even though they were banned by law in 200CE, the events continued.

A VENATOR SPEARS A
SNARLING LEOPARD

GLADIATRIX

MEN AND WOMEN ALIKE LOVED TO WATCH THE GLADIATOR SHOWS IN ANCIENT ROME. SOMETIMES A FEMALE GLADIATOR (OR GLADIATRIX) COULD EVEN BE SEEN IN COMBAT, FIGHTING FROM A CHARIOT OR WIELDING A SWORD IN THE ARENA.

A GLADIATRIX
PREPARING
TO FIGHT

KILLER WOMEN

READY FOR COMBAT

Many Roman men ridiculed the idea of women being able to fight. One of these was a famous poet called Juvenal. His writings might be sarcastic, but they do tell us how a would-be gladiatrix might train – essentially in the same way as her male colleagues. He describes how she would learn to use weapons, slashing at wooden dummies and practising her moves. She would prepare for combat by padding and bandaging herself before putting on her armour and perhaps a helmet.

WOMEN GET FIT

Pictures found in Sicily, Italy, show that about 1,700 years ago some Roman women did hard physical exercise. The mosaics show a group of ten women training as athletes. The two shown here are jumping while holding weights and practising throwing the discus. Another picture shows one of them winning a contest.

AMAZONS

This carving from Halicarnassus, now in Turkey, is the only piece of historical evidence that actually shows female gladiators in action. The stone records that these particular women were granted their freedom. One is named Amazon – a reference to the Amazons, a feared nation of female warriors from Greek legend.

FEMALE
GLADIATORS
IN ACTION

"In this contest, women took part, most fiercely, and rude comments were made about other, refined women as well. So it was forbidden for any woman to fight in single combat."

historian Dio Cassius

THE GLADIUS

This short sword was the main weapon used by Roman soldiers and also by many of the combatants in the arena, whether male or female. Its Latin name was the gladius, which is where the words gladiator and gladiatrix come from. The steel blade of the sword was about 65cm long. It had two cutting edges, so it could be used for both slashing and stabbing.

POWER BAR

SPARTAN

DATA FILE
ANCIENT GREEK HOPLITES, OR FOOT SOLDIERS, WENT INTO BATTLE FROM THE 6TH TO THE 1ST CENTURY BCE. RENOWNED AS THE TOUGHEST WERE THE LAKEDAIMONIANS, FROM THE WARLIKE CITY-STATE OF SPARTA. FIGHTING WITH SPEAR AND SHIELD, THEY WERE THE PREMIER WARRIORS OF THEIR AGE.

HOPLITE

1. CORINTHIAN HELMET
2. LONG, STRAIGHT SPEAR WITH IRON SPEAR-HEAD
3. CRIMSON-COLOURED EXOMIS (TUNIC)
4. BARE FOOT
5. BRONZE 'MUSCLE' CUIRASS (BODY ARMOUR)
6. ASPIS (CIRCULAR SHIELD) WITH WARRIOR'S PERSONAL EMBLEM

480BCE

PICK A WEAPON

SPEAR
The 2.5m-long Lakedaimonian spear is a formidable weapon. Light and strong, it can be thrust at an enemy with great force.

SWORD
Use the short sword to stab at your opponent's groin or torso. If you break your spear, this is perfect for scrappy, close-range fighting.

SHIELD
WARNING! Hoplites who lose their shield will be punished! At home, store it with the bronze arm-hole removed, as a guard against theft.

ADD STAMINA

FOOD
Spartan hoplites are trained to work on an empty stomach – get used to a lean diet of thin broth and you'll never be too weak to fight.

FIRST AID
Get your wound rinsed and sewn up with thread soaked in hot olive oil, and take a drug made from the herb dittany as pain relief.

ADVICE
Keep in shape while on campaign by practising athletic exercises, to battle music, in the morning and evening.

MAKE YOUR MOVE

ADVANCE
Move in any direction and quickly thrust, guarded behind your shield.

COUNTERSTRIKE
Cut from behind your shield while using it to deflect opposing blows.

THRUST
Step onto the rear foot to make a strong, long-reaching defensive stab.

SPARTAN

MONGOL

MONGOL

DATA FILE
MONGOL HORSEMEN RODE ACROSS ASIA IN THE 13TH AND 14TH CENTURY, STRIKING FEAR INTO THE HEARTS OF ALL THEY APPROACHED. AMONG THESE HARDY, FIT AND HIGHLY SKILLED ARCHERS WERE THE KESHIKS, FIRING THEIR ARROWS IN AN AWESOME ONSLAUGHT.

PICK A WEAPON

SABRE
A good choice if you're on horseback or on foot. The 60cm-long curved sword is used one-handed for cutting and slashing.

ARROWS
Pick large ones with broad arrowheads for close fighting so you can deliver deep, piercing wounds to your enemy's face and arms.

BOW
Use your bow to shoot arrows a long way, with power and deadly accuracy. Keep a spare bow or two in protective cases.

KESHIK

1250CE

1. BOW MADE OF YAK HORN, SINEW AND BAMBOO

2. THICK, FUR-TRIMMED HAT

3. ARROWS – 30 SMALL AND 30 LARGER ONES

4. THICK, SHEEPSKIN COAT WITH SILK SHIRT UNDERNEATH

5. STOUT LEATHER BOOTS

6. SABRE (SLIGHTLY CURVED SWORD)

MAKE YOUR MOVE

PARTING SHOT
Run away from a close-in opponent so you can increase your bow range.

HIGH WARD
Lift the sabre high to allow strong attacking slashes, and keep the shield close.

STEADY SHOT
Take time to line up an expertly aimed shot at the most vulnerable area.

FOOD
Hunt a wild marmot, fox or hare to eat with some of the hard paste made from dried mare's milk that you keep with you at all times.

FIRST AID
Mongol camps follow close behind the front line, so if injured you'll soon be given treatment and can rest, looked after by your family.

ADVICE
In daylight watch with the vigilance of a wolf, at night with the eyes of a raven, and in battle fall upon the enemy like a falcon.

ADD STAMINA

POWER BAR

SPARTAN

A STATUE OF LEONIDAS, KING OF SPARTA

GROWING UP IN THE GREEK STATE OF SPARTA WAS AS TOUGH AS IT COMES. CHILDREN LEARNED THAT THE FIRST DUTY OF EVERY ADULT CITIZEN WAS TO FIGHT SPARTA'S ENEMIES – AND SHOW NO FEAR. THE HOPLITE WAS THE SUPREME WARRIOR OF THE AGE.

SPARTAN

THE MONGOL LIES OVERPOWERED

THE SPARTAN WINS

THE MONGOL FIGHTS BEST WHEN GALLOPING ON HORSEBACK, HIS MANY ARROWS FLYING RELENTLESSLY AT THE ENEMY. THE SPARTAN IS BEST ON FIRM GROUND AS PART OF THE PHALANX, A CHARGING WALL OF SHIELDS AND SPEARS. ON FOOT, IN HAND-TO-HAND FIGHTING, THE SPARTAN HAD NO EQUAL. EVEN ON HIS OWN, OUT OF THE PHALANX, HE IS FAST AND POWERFUL AND HE FEARLESSLY BEARS DOWN ON HIS OPPONENT WITH HIS HEAVY SPEAR. AFTER ALL, HE HAS BEEN TRAINING FOR THIS MOMENT FOR MOST OF HIS LIFE.

HOPLITES IN ACTION

THERMOPYLAI

One of the most famous battles in history took place at Thermopylai, Greece, in 480BCE. For three days a small Greek army commanded by the Spartan king, Leonidas, held back one of the biggest armies the world had ever seen, assembled by the Persian king, Xerxes. A last stand was made by 300 Spartan hoplites, who fought to the bitter end. The Persians won the battle – but lost the war.

HARSH SCHOOLING

Even today, people use the word 'Spartan' to mean 'hard', 'harsh' or 'without luxury'. Girls were trained in athletics so they would be physically tough and one day have strong sons. Boys were separated from their families at the age of seven, and spent over ten years at military school, training to fight. They were expected to be cool-headed and fearless in the heat of battle.

THE PHALANX

In battle, hoplites closed ranks in a formation called the phalanx. Their shields overlapped each other, making a solid barrier. Their spears bristled forwards, preventing the enemy from fighting at close quarters. Rows of men advanced, with musicians playing to keep them in time. If the formation broke, the hoplites slashed at the enemy with their swords.

KING LEONIDAS LEADS THE SPARTANS IN A 2006 FILM ABOUT THERMOPYLAI

"STRANGER, TELL THEM IN SPARTA THAT WE LIE HERE, OBEDIENT TO THEIR COMMANDS."

GREEK POET SIMONIDES ON THE FALLEN SPARTAN HEROES BURIED AT THERMOPYLAI

BATTLE

THE BURNING OF BAGHDAD

In 1258 the biggest army in Mongol history surrounded the magnificent city of Baghdad, in what is now Iraq. The war leader of the Mongol hordes was Hulagu, grandson of Genghis Khan. The city walls were soon breached and hundreds of thousands of citizens were slaughtered as they fled. Mosques, palaces and libraries of priceless books were burned to the ground. The caliph, or ruler, of Baghdad was rolled up in a carpet and trampled to death by the hooves of the Mongol horses. Such was the price of resisting the Mongol advance.

MONGOL

THE MONGOLS WERE SUPERLATIVE HORSE-RIDERS AND DEADLY ARCHERS FROM THE STEPPES OF ASIA. THEIR ARMIES SWEPT INTO CHINA, INDIA, THE MIDDLE EAST AND RUSSIA. THEY SEEMED SUPERHUMAN AND WERE DREADED AS INVINCIBLE.

GENGHIS KHAN, AS PORTRAYED IN A 2007 FILM

LIFE ON THE STEPPES

The Mongols were nomads who travelled with their sheep, goats, camels and cattle across the vast deserts and the grasslands or steppes of east and central Asia. Mongol bands kept horses in herds numbering 10,000 or more, and relied heavily on mare's milk for their food and drink. They camped in large felt tents called gers. When on campaign, whole Mongol communities followed and supported the front-line soldiers.

HELMET AND ARMOURED COAT

ARMOUR TO PROTECT A HORSE'S HEAD

ARMOURED RIDERS

ELITE MONGOL CAVALRYMEN — AND THEIR HORSES — WORE ARMOUR OF SMALL PLATES OR SCALES, MADE OF METAL OR HARDENED LEATHER, ATTACHED TO A BACKING OF SILK OR OTHER CLOTH. IT NEEDED TO BE LIGHT ENOUGH TO WEAR ON LONG AND EXHAUSTING MANOEUVRES, AND TOUGH ENOUGH TO REPEL ENEMY ARROWS.

MONGOL HORSEMEN AT FULL CHARGE

GENGHIS KHAN

Mobility and endurance were the keys to the Mongols' success in battle. Their tough, stocky horses could gallop at speed, wheeling round, withdrawing and then regrouping to charge once more. Weapons included the sabre, the hooked lance and a powerful bow. A hail of arrows would devastate enemy troops before a charge. In 1206 the Mongols united under a brilliant war leader called Temujin (1162–1227). He became known as Genghis Khan ('ruler of all'). His capital was at Karakorum, in Mongolia, but his armies fanned out to attack China, Central Asia, Persia and Russia.

FIVE VICTORS

OUR PAIRS OF WARRIORS, SEPARATED BY CENTURIES AND VAST DISTANCES, NEVER MET IN REAL LIFE. SO HOW DO WE KNOW WHO HAS WON? EACH IS SHAPED BY TRAINING, FIGHTING STYLE, WEAPONS, IDEALS, AND MENTAL AND PHYSICAL STRENGTH. IN HISTORY, MANY FACTORS INFLUENCED THEIR SUCCESSES: ARMY SIZE AND ORGANIZATION, TACTICS, TECHNOLOGY AND EVEN WEATHER. IN OUR CONTESTS, EACH IS ON FOOT, IN SINGLE COMBAT, IN AN ARENA. WE CAN WORK OUT WHAT IS LIKELY TO HAVE HAPPENED, BUT EACH WARRIOR IS AN INDIVIDUAL. WHATEVER THE WEAPONS AND FIGHTING STYLE, INDIVIDUAL SKILL IS CRUCIAL TO THE OUTCOME.

WINNER: KNIGHT
The knight is heavily armed and his swordsmanship at close quarters is exceptional. The Zulu, despite being fast and agile and a skilled spear-fighter, is not well prepared for single combat. In history, knights faced many different enemies and adapted their fighting style to beat them.

WINNER: NINJA
The ninja beats the gladiatrix. Unlike gladiators, ninja were not trained for prolonged combat. They were tough, skilled with many weapons, used cunning and surprise, and always intended to kill.

WINNER: SAMURAI
The samurai is a disciplined, well-equipped warrior who fights well on foot. The gladiator is not a soldier but a performer who looks to the crowd to decide his fate. In history, the samurai resisted invasion by the Mongols.

THE KNIGHT

THE KNIGHT IS STRONGER THAN THE OTHER VICTORS. HE HAS THE WIDEST VARIETY OF DUELLING SKILLS AND WEAPONS. HIS LIFELONG TRAINING, WARLIKE MENTALITY AND WARRIOR CODE GIVE HIM THE EDGE OVER ANYONE. HE HAS LEARNED FROM OTHER KNIGHTS' EXPERIENCE OF FACING DIVERSE ENEMIES. HE IS OUR ULTIMATE WINNER.

WINNER: SPARTAN

The Spartan is in his element in foot combat and is used to facing light archer opponents. He is fast and powerful. The Mongol is part of a formidable army, but on his own, on foot, he is not strong or fast enough to compete, and is too close to fire his arrows effectively.

WINNER: VIKING

The Viking wins glory by slaying opponents. Aztecs win honour by capturing an enemy ready for sacrifice later – so the jaguar warrior is hampered by his approach. In history the Aztecs were defeated altogether because their code of war was so different from that of their European conquerors.

WINNER HEAD TO TOE

 HELMET – others give good protection, but the knight's hinged visor allows good visibility too.

 WEAPON – the knight's personal weaponry, evolved over hundreds of years, is excellent for duelling. His sword is his best weapon.

ARMOUR – the knight's armour is better even than that of the samurai, Aztec, Spartan and Mongol.

MIND – the knight trains to think quickly and respond strongly in any fight.

SPIRIT – all warriors have fighting spirit, but the knight's is a deadly combination of his skills, equipment, ideals and experience.

RE-MATCHES

WE'VE FOUND OUR FIVE VICTORS AND OUR ULTIMATE
WINNER. BUT WOULD THINGS HAVE BEEN DIFFERENT IF
THE CONTESTS HAD BEEN BETWEEN DIFFERENT PAIRS?
WHAT DO YOU THINK? WHOSE WEAPONS ARE BEST?
WHO IS MOST SKILLED? WHO HAS THE MENTAL EDGE?

AZTEC VS SAMURAI

The Aztec swings his vicious macuahuitl at the
samurai's limbs. His shield and cotton armour give
him good protection, but can he really compete with
the weapons and swordsmanship of the samurai? The
samurai will win honour from killing or dying. The
Aztec is prepared to die, but not hungry to kill.

WINNER: YOU DECIDE...

VIKING VS GLADIATRIX

The gladiatrix punches forwards with her shield while
readying her dagger to strike. But she is used to an
opponent of equal strength and a fixed-length fight,
not a battle to the death against a beefy, ferocious
warrior who has killed many enemies before. Her
head is unprotected. Who will triumph?

WINNER: YOU DECIDE...

SPARTAN VS ZULU

Both warriors fight with shield and spear – ancient yet effective weapons adapted for their own fighting styles. Both have trained from boyhood, and in both cultures to be a man is to be a warrior. But which has the toughest training regime and the best physical condition, the deadliest focus and the better armour?

WINNER: YOU DECIDE...

GLADIATOR VS KNIGHT

The gladiator is strong and heavy, his shield is large and his helmet gives good protection, so he can defend himself well. But can he hope to find a chink in his opponent's armour or compete with the knight's array of precise and deadly duelling moves? Surely it's just a matter of time before the game is up?

WINNER: YOU DECIDE...

MONGOL VS NINJA

Both have terrifying reputations. The Mongol is clumsy on foot, but his sabre is a good choice for close combat. The ninja is mentally agile and moves with strength and speed. But she has no armour, whereas his thick coat and silk shirt can stop and hold a piercing blade. Who will manage to deliver the fatal blow?

WINNER: YOU DECIDE...

AZTEC

ATLATL (ot-la-t) A spear-thrower consisting of a stick carved with special loops for the fingers that is used to launch darts or spears.

CONQUISTADORES The Spanish forces who invaded and conquered several native American peoples including the Aztecs.

ELITE The most powerful, talented, successful or richest members of a society. Elite warriors are those who have achieved high status through success in battle.

EMPIRE A group of lands and nations governed by a single ruler.

FLOWER WAR A battle waged by the Aztecs to train soldiers and to capture prisoners for sacrifice. It was a young soldier's first battle.

MACUAHUITL (ma-kwa-wheat) Aztec saw-sword.

OBSIDIAN A glass-like volcanic substance that occurs naturally in Mexico.

PARRY A move to block or deflect an attack.

SACRIFICE The killing of a living thing as an offering to the gods.

TEMPLE A building dedicated to a god or goddess and used for rituals, festivals or offerings.

VIKING

BERSERKER A particular type of Viking warrior, especially fierce and violent.

BOSS A round metal knob, e.g. covering the hand-grip of a shield.

CULT A system of religious belief, often an extreme version of a more widespread religion, with particular beliefs and customs. An example is the berserker cult.

FRENZIED In a state of violent excitement.

JARL (yarl) Scandinavian regional ruler or chieftain, usually one level below a king.

LETHAL Deadly.

LITHSMAN An ordinary, freeborn Viking warrior.

MEAD An alcoholic drink made from honey.

PLUNDER To steal people's goods and possessions by force, e.g. in a raid or attack.

PROW The front part of a ship.

SCABBARD The piece of equipment in which a sword is stored when not in use.

SCANDINAVIA The geographical region that includes modern-day Norway, Sweden, Denmark and Iceland.

GLADIATOR

AMPHITHEATRE An oval or circular stadium where Roman audiences watched gladiator fights and other sporting events.

ARENA The central, sand-covered part of an amphitheatre, where fights were staged.

BARRACKS A complex of buildings where soldiers – or gladiators – lived and trained.

GLADIUS The ancient Roman short sword, used by soldiers and by gladiators.

LANISTA The head and owner of a school of gladiators.

LUDUS Gladiator school.

MURMILLO A type of gladiator who wore a crested helmet.

RETIARIUS A type of gladiator who fought with a trident

(three-pointed spear), net and dagger.

SECUTOR A type of gladiator specially equipped to fight a retiarius.

SLAVE A person who is deprived of freedom and rights, can be bought and sold, and is forced to work for no reward.

VISOR The movable part of a helmet that covers the face.

SAMURAI

BUSHIDO The samurai code of honour or 'way of the warrior'. It included the principles of justice and honesty, contempt for death, self-control, politeness, loyalty to superiors and a duty to defend the honour of one's name.

DAIMYO [dye-myow] A samurai leader or warlord.

DO Samurai body armour, made of leather straps or scales, joined together with silk or leather cord.

HARI-KIRI A method of ritual suicide carried out by samurai warriors . It means 'stomach-cutting'.

KATANA The long samurai sword.

MEDIEVAL Belonging to a period of history from approximately the 6th to the 16th century CE.

NOBLE Belonging to the nobility, a high level of society.

SHOGUN A Japanese military leader.

TANTO Samurai dagger.

TORSO The top part of a person's body – the chest, stomach and back.

YARI Spear used by samurai and by Japanese foot-soldiers.

KNIGHT

CHIVALRY The knight's code of honour.

COAT-OF-ARMS A badge worn by a knight on his shield or clothing to identify him in battle.

COURTEOUS Polite, considerate and respectful.

CRUSADES The series of 'holy' wars, from 1095 to 1291CE, launched by Christian Europe for control of the parts of the Middle East known as the Holy Land.

DUEL A fight between two people (also called single combat).

EARL A type of knight – rich, a great landowner and minor royal.

MACE A heavy, spiked club.

MAIL Armour made from many small, interlinked iron rings.

POLEAXE A type of battleaxe with a hammerhead and spike as its head.

SIEGE An attempt to force a castle or town to surrender or be captured by cutting off its supplies and communications and by attacking its defences.

TOURNAMENT A pageant where knights fought mock battles, to practise and show off their fighting skills.

BATTLEAXES
Warriors have used versions of this ancient tool in battle for thousands of years. Cheaper than swords, battleaxes can be swung or thrown. Look out for the variety in axe-heads.

SWORDS
A sword is a long metal blade with a sharpened edge or edges, and a point. Design and technique vary, but for many cultures this is the weapon that is most highly prized.

DAGGERS
These weapons developed from prehistoric tools. Shorter than swords, and easier to conceal, they are useful stabbing weapons for use in close combat.

WEAPONS

WARRIOR WORDS

ZULU

AFRIKANER A South African person descended from Dutch settlers.

IBUTHO (plural: ambutho) A regiment of 1,000 Zulu warriors. Each had its own shield colours, and often it contained warriors who were all the same age, and had trained together since boyhood.

IKLWA A Zulu stabbing spear.

IMPI The Zulu word for any group of armed fighters, for example an army, made up of many ambutho.

INYANGA (plural: isinyanga) Zulu healer or traditional herbal doctor.

IQAWE A great hero renowned among Zulu warriors.

ISIJULA Throwing spear, used for hunting as well as in battle.

IWISA A club (sometimes called a knobkerrie) used for delivering heavy blows to the head.

RATIONS The amount of food issued to soldiers when they are on active service.

RITUAL A formal action, performed in a particular and usually solemn way, e.g. for a religious purpose.

NINJA

ASSASSIN Someone who kills secretly or by surprise.

GEISHA A traditional Japanese female entertainer, who dances and plays music to entertain men.

HOKODE Hand claws, used for climbing walls and for fighting.

KUNOICHI A female ninja.

KUSARIGAMA Ninja weapon consisting of a long chain linking a sickle to a heavy ball.

MARTIAL ARTS Any of a group of styles of fighting and self-defence. Japanese examples include kendo, ju-jitsu, judo and karate.

NINJUTSU The 'art of stealth' or of being a ninja. Its 18 disciplines included unarmed combat, sword fighting, disguise and impersonation, espionage (spying) and geography.

SHURIKEN Throwing star – a star-shaped arrangement of blades to be used as a missile.

SICKLE A curve-bladed implement used in farming for cutting crops, and which also makes a dangerous weapon.

TESSEN A fan concealing blades among its folds.

YAM An edible root, a bit like a potato.

GLADIATRIX

AMAZON A member of a tribe of female warriors from ancient Greek legend.

ANUBIS The ancient Egyptian god of burial and funerals, thought to protect the dead and lead their souls to the afterlife. In ancient Rome, Anubis and Mercury (in some ways a Roman equivalent) were associated with gladiators. People dressed as Mercury would carry fallen gladiators from the arena.

CELT A member of a group of peoples who lived in central Europe some time before 800BCE. The Celts were some of the Romans' most hated and feared enemies.

CHARIOT A horse-drawn, two-wheeled cart used in ancient warfare or for racing.

MOSAIC A picture or design made from small pieces of coloured glass or stone. Many surviving Roman mosaics include pictures of gladiators.

NUBIAN A person from the ancient kingdom of Nubia (now part of Egypt and Sudan), which lay just beyond the Roman empire.

VENATOR A type of gladiator who fought against wild beasts such as big cats. He fought with a spear.

SPEARS

A spear is a simple but effective weapon. Made from a wooden shaft and a sharp metal head, it can be short or long, thrown like a javelin or used close-range to thrust.

SHIELDS

These hand-held weapons are used offensively, hitting hard with the edge or centre, and defensively, to deflect and block enemy blows. Look for the variety in shape and design.

BOWS

A bow is a spring for firing arrows. The archer draws (pulls back on) the string of the bow, storing energy that powers the arrow forwards, far and fast.

SPARTAN

CITIZEN A member of a city.

CITY-STATE A city that is also an independent state. Ancient Greece was made up of city-states including Athens, Corinth, Sparta and Thebes.

CUIRASS Body armour, often made of bronze, worn by Greek soldiers to protect the torso.

EMBLEM A picture, design or badge worn by a warrior.

EXOMIS A particular type of tunic worn by Spartan hoplites. Spartans usually wore crimson tunics in battle – for them, crimson was a manly, warlike colour and an honourable choice because the dye was expensive.

HOPLITE Ancient Greek foot-soldier, armed with spear and shield. Named after the Greek word for shield, hoplon.

LAKEDAIMONIAN Another word for Spartan. Originally Sparta was the capital city of a state called Lakedaimonia, but the state itself became known as Sparta, too.

PHALANX A battle formation used by Greek hoplites. It consisted of eight ranks of men, each lined up with their shields locked together to form a wall. The front three lines held their spears ready for attack.

MONGOL

ARCHER A person who shoots with a bow and arrows.

CAVALRY Soldiers who fight on horseback.

GER A Mongol portable house (often called by its Turkish name of yurt). It is a circular tent made of a wooden framework covered in felt.

HORDE A Mongol field army.

INVINCIBLE Unbeatable.

KESHIK A Mongol light archer. About six out of every ten Mongol troops were keshiks.

LANCE A type of spear.

MANOEUVRE A large-scale military movement such as an attack by an army.

NOMAD One of a group of people who have no fixed home or town but live in temporary camps and move from place to place.

PERSIANS The people of the vast Persian empire, centred on modern-day Iran.

QUIVER The container in which an archer stores his arrows.

STEPPE A vast area of grassland stretching from eastern Europe across central Asia.

INDEX

In this index, 'data page' refers to the page of information about each warrior that folds out from each combat scene.

First published 2009 by Kingfisher
an imprint of Macmillan Children's Books
a division of Macmillan Publishers Limited
4 Crinan Street, London N1 9XW
Basingstoke and Oxford
Associated companies throughout the world
www.panmacmillan.com

CONCEPT BY Hannah Wilson
WRITTEN BY Catherine Brereton, Philip Steele, Hannah Wilson
ILLUSTRATION BY Steve Stone, represented by Artist Partners Ltd.
DESIGN BY Jo Connor

CONSULTANTS: Dr Hugh Bowden, King's College London; John Clements, Association for Renaissance Martial Arts; Professor Peter Heather, King's College London; Ian Knight; Dr John M D Pohl, UCLA; Dr Stephen Turnbull, Leeds University

ISBN 978-0-7534-1908-3

1 3 5 7 9 8 6 4 2

1TR/0609/SC/LFA/157MA/C

A CIP catalogue record for this book
is available from the British Library.

Printed in China

THE PUBLISHER WOULD LIKE TO THANK THE FOLLOWING FOR PERMISSION TO REPRODUCE THEIR MATERIAL.

Every care has been taken to trace copyright holders. However, if there have been unintentional omissions or failure to trace copyright holders, we apologize and will, if informed, endeavour to make corrections in any future edition.
(t = top, b = bottom, c = centre, l = left, r = right):

Pages 4bl Shutterstock/Kateryna Potrokova; 12tl Shutterstock/LoopAll; 12bl National Geographic Society/Ted Spiegel; 12br with the kind permission of the British Museum Board of Trustees; 13tc with the kind permission of the British Museum Board of Trustees; 13tr Alamy/Homer Sykes; 13c Alamy/Troy GB Images; 13b S.H.E Production, Canada; 15tl Art Archive/National History Museum, Mexico City; 15tr Art Archive/Museum fur Volkerkunde, Vienna; 15cr with the kind permission of the British Museum Board of Trustees; 15bl Getty/Moritz Steiger; 15br Corbis/Lake County Museum; 22 Alamy/Japan Art Collection; 23tr Alamy/Malcolm Fairman; 23bl Alamy/Photos12; 24l Getty/DK; 24cl Scala/National Museum, Naples; 24br Alamy/Jochen Tack; 25t Corbis/Roger Wood; 25bl Alamy/Content Mine International; 25cr Shutterstock/PixAchi; 25 Rex Features, 32bl Photolibrary/Stephan Goerlich; 32–33 Arena Artists Partners; 33ct Getty/Robert Harding; 33c Art Archive/Musee Conde Chantilly; 33br Heritage Images/The Board of Trustees of the Armouries, Leeds; 34cl Bridgeman Art Library (BAL)/Heini Schneebeli; 34bl BAL/Heini Schneebeli; 34bl BAL/Heini Schneebeli; 34bl Alamy/Interfoto; 34bl BAL/Heini Schneebeli; 34r Art Archive; 35tl Alamy/Dennis Cox; 35b Alamy/Zute Lightfoot; 42bl Stephen Turnbull; 42cb Alamy/Interfoto; 43t Getty/Aurora Images, 43c Getty/Aurora Images, 43tr Alamy/Iain Masterton; 43cl Shutterstock/Lilun; 43bl Rex Features; 44tl Corbis/Alinari; 44bl Alamy/Nick Turner; 44r Alamy/Nick Turner; 45tc Alamy/Photos12; 45tr with the kind permission of the British Museum Board of Trustees; 45bl Alamy/Nick Turner; 45r Rex Features/Solent News; 52tr Alamy/Rolf Richardson; 53tl Shutterstock/Petros Tsonis; 53tl Alamy/The London Art Archive; 53cl Art Archive/Archaeological Museum, Naples/Dagli Orti; 53b Ronald Grant Archive; 53br Kobal/Warner Bros; 54tl Art Archive/Bibliotheque National, Paris; 54bl Rex Features/Picturehouse/Everett; 55tl Kobal/Igor Vereschagin; 55tc Scala/Metropolitan Museum, New York; 55tr The Board of Trustees of the Armouries, Leeds; 55br Corbis/Hamid Sardar;